KOKO THE KITE

Om KIDZ
An imprint of Om Books International

Om Kidz | Om Books International

Reprinted in 2026

Corporate & Editorial Office
A-12, Sector 64, Noida 201 301
Uttar Pradesh, India
Phone: +91 120 477 4100
Email: editorial@ombooks.com
Website: www.ombooksinternational.com

Sales Office
107, Ansari Road, Darya Ganj
New Delhi 110 002, India
Phone: +91 11 4000 9000
Email: sales@ombooks.com
Website: www.ombooks.com

ISBN: 978-93-84119-49-2

Printed in India

10 9 8 7 6 5

KOKO THE KITE

I'm all set to read

Paste your photograph here

My name is

____

Koko the kite was just so good looking! All the other kites wished that they were as pretty as him. He had a long, lovely tail and was made of bright, strong, colourful paper.

Jackie, the boy who owned Koko, loved him dearly.

He took great care of Koko and made sure that nothing would spoil him. He would pack him up carefully every evening, so that he would not get torn by anything.

On windy days, Jackie would take Koko and fly him high up in the sky. Koko would soar above all the kites, feeling very proud of himself.

One day, Koko was flying proudly in the sky.

"I am flying so high, I'm sure no one can catch up with me," thought Koko. Just then, a bird flew past him. The bird just looked at Koko and shook its head in pity.

“I feel sorry for you,” said the bird. Koko was confused. No one ever pitied him. Most of them envied him. This was strange. After all, wasn’t he the strongest and the most beautiful of them all? Couldn’t he fly higher than all the other kites?

"What do you mean by that?" Koko asked the bird. "I'm the best kite in the neighbourhood! I can cut the strings of all the other kites around me. And you say you are sorry for me?" Koko was upset.

"Yes," said the bird. "That's because you can't be free." I fly wherever I want. You are tied to a string. You can fly only when someone decides to fly you. The bird flew away.

Koko wanted to be free too. "That bird is right," he said to himself. "I can fly only if Jackie holds my strings. Oh, how I would love to fly away on my own." And suddenly, Koko got an idea.

That day, when Koko was flying among the other kites, he flew right into the middle of a kite fight. Strings were at war and twang! His string was cut off. Koko flew up in the air and away from Jackie.

"I'm free, I'm free," Koko sang to himself as he soared in the skies. Higher and higher he went. There was no string to hold him back this time. He flew over rivers and hills. He saw cows grazing below. He flew so high that he touched the clouds!

Suddenly, the wind dropped. WHOOOOSH! Koko found himself falling. Down, down, down he went and plop! He landed on the ground. "Ouch," said Koko. He had never fallen down before.

Koko looked around in fear. This had never happened to him before. Jackie was always around to look after him when the wind stopped. In fact, Jackie always made sure that Koko landed gently and softly without ever getting scratched or torn.

Just then, a huge wet nose sniffed Koko. It was a cow. She was wondering if she could eat Koko. He was terrified! But the cow changed her mind and went away. A kite didn't smell as nice as the fresh green grass on the other side of the fence.

Koko had hardly heaved a sigh of relief when he felt himself being turned over. He felt two sharp things poking him and strange whiskers tickling him.

"Mew mew," said two little kittens as they pawed Koko's tail. They thought he was something to play with! They pulled Koko's lovely tail and frisked happily around him. Now kittens, as you know, love to play. These kittens loved Koko and his lovely long tail.

Koko curled up in fright. He was sure that the kittens were going to tear him up into shreds. He had heard that kittens had sharp claws and he had even felt them.

“Kitty! Kitty!” someone called. Luckily for Koko, the little kittens ran away, leaving him safe on the ground. “The kite was a lovely thing to play with,” thought the kittens. “But it’s not half as nice as the bowl of milk we’ll get at home.”

Koko was miserable. "I wish I hadn't gotten in the middle of that kite fight," he thought sadly. He thought about how much Jackie loved him and felt very sorry indeed. He thought of how safe he was with Jackie. He really missed him.

At that moment, Koko heard a sound.

THUD THUD THUD THUD. PUTT PUTT PUTT PUTT. What a scary sound that was! Poor Koko was terrified.

"Oh no!" Koko knew that sound. It was the lawn mower that Jackie's father often used. It tore and ate up everything that came in its way. It ate up grass, leaves, bits of paper and just about anything!

Koko was truly scared. He was sure that this time, he was going to be torn and eaten up by the lawn mower. This was even worse than being torn by the cow or the kittens. Just then, he felt himself being raised off the ground.

Two strong talons got hold of his colourful paper. “What was that?” thought Koko, thoroughly frightened. He loved being up in the sky, but not if he was being held so tight by such a nasty-looking bird.

It was an eagle, who had decided that Koko was just what he needed to make his nest nice and colourful. Koko was miserable. Imagine him spending the rest of his life in a little nest with baby eagles all around him! By now, he was feeling very sorry that he had cut himself off.

At that moment, there was a loud sound. The eagle was startled. It was a clap of thunder. That was followed by flashes of lightning across the sky. The eagle forgot all about Koko and dropped him.

Koko fell down. He wondered where he was going to land. He hoped that no cow, kitten or eagle would get him this time. Suddenly, he landed with a plop in someone's garden. Koko lay there helplessly, wondering what would happen to him.

He heard a cow mooing. He heard a kitten mewing. He heard footsteps running up to him. And then, he heard a voice that he loved so much. "Look, my kite has returned!" It was his very own Jackie, who came running and picked Koko lovingly.

Koko couldn't believe his luck. He had flown far and wide. He'd almost been eaten up, mowed over and torn. He had adventures that he hadn't liked one little bit. But he was safe now, because he was at home with Jackie.

That night, as Jackie placed Koko safely upon the cupboard, Koko realised that he didn't want to be a bird. He was a beautiful kite and he was happiest flying safely at the end of a string. He never tried to fly away again.

If you look high in the sky and see a lovely blue, red, yellow and green kite flying happily away, you will know who that is. It's Koko, of course. He's happy to be with Jackie. And he's happy to be the most handsome kite in the skies.